Most writers will find what I have to say in this short book difficult to hear. Many writers have already refused to believe me. I've watched several close their eyes and pretend what I'm saying isn't true. Unfortunately, those folks will cease making money at their writing in the next five years. These writers will fall by the wayside—and I see that as a tragedy.

But the ones who recognize that the change is happening are the ones who are going to survive in this new world of publishing. They might make choices I disagree with, but they'll make those choices out of knowledge rather than ignorance. As a fellow writer—and more importantly, as a reader—that's all I can ask.

Surviving the Transition

How Writers Can Thrive in the New World of Publishing

Kristine Kathryn Rusch

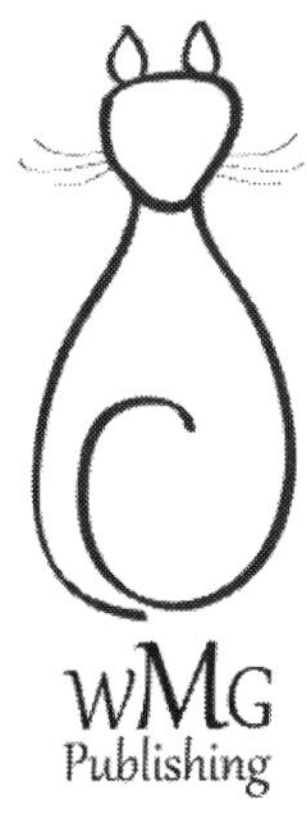

More Business Books by

Kristine Kathryn Rusch

The Freelancer's Survival Guide (full book)

Freelancer's Survival Guide Short Books

When to Quit Your Day Job
Getting Started
Turning Setbacks into Opportunity
Goals and Dreams
How to Negotiate Anything
The Secrets of Success
How to Make Money
Networking in Person and Online
Time Management

Surviving the Transition

Published 2012 by WMG Publishing
www.wmgpublishing.com

WMG Publishing
www.wmgpublishing.com

Table of Contents

Surviving the Transition

How Writers Can Thrive in the New World of Publishing

Kristine Kathryn Rusch

Introduction

I first wrote the following short book as a series of blog posts at the end of April 2011. Publishing was—and still is—changing so fast that only the most aware can keep up. Established writers, working under deadline, literally live in their own fantasy worlds. When it comes time to market a new book or fulfill an option book, when it comes time to negotiate a new contract with a publisher, these writers will emerge from their fantasy world into a place they don't understand.

The problem is that it will look just like the place they left when they began their most recent project. These writers won't often know that they're in a new world until it's too late.

I wrote this short book as a wake-up call. "Writing Like It's 1999" is still the most-read post on my blog. Maybe the wake-up call is working.

I hope so.

I want my colleagues to do well. I want them to have the best careers they can possibly have in this new century, and that means understanding where the business is now.

Most writers will find what I have to say in this short book difficult to hear. Many writers have already refused to believe me. I've watched several close their eyes and pretend what I'm saying isn't true. Unfortunately, those folks will cease making money at their writing in the next five years. These writers will fall by the wayside—and I see that as a tragedy.

But the ones who recognize that the change is happening are the ones who are going to survive in this new world of publishing. They might make choices I disagree with, but they'll make those choices out of knowledge rather than ignorance. As a fellow writer—and more importantly, as a reader—that's all I can ask.

I hope this short volume helps you in your career, whatever path you might take.

—Kristine Kathryn Rusch
Lincoln City, Oregon
January 7, 2012

Writing Like It's 1999

When change hits in the arts, it hits hard. Recently, I was reading an article in the April 2011 *Vanity Fair Magazine* about the movie *All The President's Men*. The last two paragraphs of the article discuss how, in 1975, Sidney Sheinberg at MCA came up with a new way to release movies. Once upon a time, folks, movies released slowly, one or two theaters at a time, and worked their way across the country. It meant that the studio had to make fewer copies of the film, and that movies could become "sleepers"—films that actually built word of mouth over time.

Sheinberg decided to amortize costs by sending hundreds of prints of the film to theaters all over the country, and to run a nationwide advertising campaign at the same time. The movie he chose to do this with? *Jaws*.

That little idea changed the way movies got marketed—and did so damn near overnight. *All the President's Men* got released just after *Jaws*, while this system was still in flux.

"*Jaws* was a good, populist movie," Robert Redford, star of *All the President's Men*, said. "But it became the flagship for a campaign that overtook American movies. It became a slick package, advertising-directed, about selling popcorn and product placement. I thought the timing of *All the President's Men* very fortunate, because it was a very honest and unpolluted film. I'm not sure if we could have managed it in its purity a decade or two later."

Over the years, Redford has fascinated me because he has always had one foot in the business world even as he built his artistic career. He started the Sundance Film Festival when it became clear that the smaller films—which *All the President's Men* was—had no shot in the changing market. The festival helped give films like that, films that didn't have the benefit of timing, a shot.

Why am I talking about movies here? Because I want you to see the rapidity of change in the film industry. A marketing and business decision that was quite wise from a studio's point of view ended up having a major impact on the kinds of films that got produced, distributed, and sold to film audiences. Say what you will about the auteurs in the 1970s, most of them wouldn't have had a chance had they started in the 1990s. And it had nothing to do with their talent.

It had to do with the way the business had changed.

The publishing industry is going through the exact same kind of rapid change. It's extremely fast—so fast that that I now give out different advice to newer writers than I would have given them just a year before.

Writers have to learn business and they have to learn the *new* business. If they don't, they'll go by the wayside quickly.

I'm worried about this. And I've been worried that my friends and fellow established writers aren't moving with me. Here's why:

It has become increasingly clear to me that the publishing industry is making changes that emulate the music industry. Those of us who exist on the periphery of the music industry have heard for years that new artists and even established ones can't make money in the traditional music industry.

I didn't understand that until I read Jacob Slichter's *So You Wanna Be A Rock N Roll Star* several years ago. He wrote about a system in which a musician who signed a deal with a major record label could end up *owing* the label tens if not hundreds of thousands of dollars. He delineated it all out in a long book that showed just how the label ended up taking a naïve artist and putting him into debt.

Slichter said this was why so many rock bands disbanded—because the band itself was a legal entity and as a legal entity it was in hock to the studio. The only way the musicians could continue to perform and try to earn money from their music was to create a new legal entity and abandon the old one. Otherwise, they were working in a kind of indentured servitude.

Think this is just sour grapes from one musician who didn't make it big? A rock producer named Steve Albini discussed it back in the 1990s in a magazine, *Maximum Rock 'n' Roll,* which I hadn't heard of before a reader sent me to a link. (For those of you who want to read the entire article, you can find it at negativland.com/albini.) In an article titled, "The Problem With Music," Albini lays out the line-by-line "costs" that the musicians agreed to when they signed their record deal. The musicians received a $250,000 advance. But by the time the album got released and the tour was completed, the advance was gone—and the musicians owed the record label $14,000.

You're understanding me right. The "standard" contractually negotiated costs that the musicians agreed would come out of their pockets came to $264,000. The only way for the artists to recoup that loss was to sign a new deal with the label, often at lesser terms. If the label even wanted to sign them. (That part is courtesy of Slichter)

How much did the label earn—with the same costs deducted?

$710,000. In 1990s dollars.

Albini also lists how much each "player" made. He includes a producer ($90,000), a manager ($51,000), an agent, ($7500) and a lawyer ($12,000).

He writes, "The band is now ¼ of the way through its contract, has made the music industry more than 3 million dollars richer, but is in the hole $14,000 in royalties. The band members have each earned about 1/3 as much as they would working at a 7-11, but they got to ride in a tour bus for a month. The next album will be about the same, except that the record company will insist they spend more time and money on it. Since the previous one never 'recouped,' the band will have no leverage and will oblige."

When I read Slichter's book, I thought, "Thank God publishing hasn't figured out how to do this to writers."

Well, folks, guess what. Publishing has figured it out.

The day I wrote this, as I looked over yet another contract addendum for a friend—this addendum sent by a big-name agent who *didn't even bother to check the addendum against the original contract terms*—I saw the agency rider added into my friend's contract. The agency rider—the thing that says the writer authorizes the publishing house to negotiate with and pay the agent in the writer's name—was awful. My friend had edited it down to something similar to what was offered ten years ago, but I know dozens of writers who probably never did.

Writers are signing away their rights, just like the musicians listed above did, because these writers aren't savvy enough to understand industry change and how it impacts art. (Like Redford mentioned in that above quote.)

Once upon a time, publishing was a monopoly. I've used this chart before. From about 1920 to about 2006, this is how publishing worked:

Writers provide content (product) to **Publishers.**
Publishers distribute that content to **Distributors**.
Distributors distribute books to **Bookstores.**
Bookstores distribute that content to **Readers**.

Now, however, writers can do this:

Writers provide content (product) to **Bookstores**
Bookstores distribute that content to **Readers**

The middleman is no longer necessary.

Many writers find this scary. They don't understand that they are—and *always have been*—in business. So they don't act like business owners.

Business owners invest capital up front to start a business. They recoup that investment over time and eventually earn money from that investment.

When publishers started paying advances, they—in effect—told writers not to bother their pretty little heads with business. "Write," the publishers said. "We'll take care of your bills while you finish that book."

Writers got used to this. Writers forgot that they had to take risks of their own *like other small business owners*. And right now, that attitude is biting writers in the ass—and most of them don't even realize it.

I write a blog called *The Business Rusch* on my website, kristinekathrynrusch.com. The blog focuses on the changes in the publishing industry from the writer's perspective. As I wrote my posts in 2011, I got e-mails and private comments from long-time professional writer friends, which, in effect, say things like, "We need agents. We can't market our books otherwise."

Or,

"Publishers are the only ones who can get us into national bookstore chains."

Or,

"I have no way to reach foreign markets/Hollywood/the gaming industry without my agent."

And you know what? Ten years ago, *that was all true*.

Publishers had a monopoly on distribution. Unless a writer became a full-fledged publisher, invested tens of thousands of dollars on a single book, and knew how to work the system, the writer could not get his book into a bookstore. How do I know this? I owned a publishing company twenty years ago. I *know* how hard it used to be. I remember the footwork my husband Dean Wesley Smith used to do to get one bookstore, two, five, or ten, on board. It was labor-intensive. He courted distributors for *years* before one took on our company.

It's not that way any more. Now, I can reach you with a blog. I can take the novel I finished on Monday, pay a savvy editor to go over the book, pay a copy editor to make sure I don't change my main character's name midway through, pay a cover designer to make me a lovely cover—all for a *flat fee*—and put the book up in two major national bookstores by the end of the week. One of those bookstores has sister stores in the U.K., Spain, France, Italy, and Germany, with more countries on the way.

Of course, this is an e-book. Putting up an e-book is spectacularly easy—and suddenly you have a worldwide market. If you're willing to go to other distributors, you can have your book in more than 20 major national bookstores within two weeks.

If I spend about $50 on CreateSpace and add a small fee for my cover designer to design a wrap-around (front and back) cover, I can have a trade paper edition of my book that will be listed in the catalogues of major distributors. I don't have to do anything else. I don't have to court those people for years, like Dean did twenty years ago.

And if I'm really willing to put myself out by designing a small catalogue of my work, I can send that to independent booksellers, give them a discount, and have CreateSpace produce and send them the paper books.

And suddenly, I am a publisher—with as great an ability to reach the consumer as any of the so-called Big Six publishers. In fact, I can reach more readers because I control *all* of the rights, and I can opt to go into overseas markets that they can't penetrate.

The monopoly isn't just broken. It's shattered.

Most writers don't realize that. Most don't want to do the "work" because they don't know how little work they have to do.

What, really, must they do? They must pay someone *up front* instead of letting that person take a percentage of the work in perpetuity.

So, let's discuss agents because that, too, is important.

Once upon a time, I had an agent. Hell, I've had a lot of agents. And I needed them.

Every writer did.

In the days before the Internet, before the ubiquity of e-mail, before instant messaging and Skype, agents had a purpose. Writers hired agents for their connections. Agents got books in the door with a reluctant publisher. Agents found partner agents overseas. Agents got into Hollywood studios.

And writers paid the agent for those connections. Writers, essentially, needed an agent to open all the closed and locked doors.

Some writers, salespeople all, did the work themselves. They booked a trip to New York, managed to get into the editor's offices, and got their work looked at.

But those writers were rare.

Then the Internet came along. And web pages. And e-mail.

The doors became open. All that secret information that agents got—which editor was buying what, who edits for the biggest publishing house in France, what's the name of the literary scout for such-n-so studio—could be Googled.

What's more, if you had a successful book or, hell, even a midlist book on a hot topic (say, vampires), then the foreign editors and the Hollywood scouts came looking for you.

On the Internet.

Through your e-mail.

I get letters all the time from interested foreign publishers and from movie people. I just closed an option deal last week with an independent producer who found me through my website.

And that is not unusual.

It's now a myth, an old and tired myth, that you need agents to open these doors. In fact, agents will often close the doors by believing that if some young producer is interested in Property A, then the agent can leverage that interest with a studio so that the studio will pay big money for Property A. I've had agents promise that kind of thing all the time, and it has never panned out.

But since I stopped using agents on my Hollywood nibbles—guess what? I have Hollywood deals. When I was agented, I only had one option in twenty years.

Now I have options running all the time.

Because of access.

And because I'm making my own decision. And because I *do* worry my formerly pretty little head about these things.

Most of my colleagues do not realize that the industry has changed, that everything they learned when they were starting out no longer applies. They don't realize that the *business* part of their industry has changed dramatically, that the deals they're signing, the people they're working with, would fit just as easily into the music industry of the 1990s.

Here's the flat truth of it, my friends: If you are a midlist writer and you sign a traditional publishing contract with most modern terms, and you do so with an agent—and not an IP attorney—negotiating for you, you will not make any more than your advance on that book. And the advance is not enough to live on. You will not be able to reserve e-book rights. Those rights will be a percentage of net, which in most contracts is undefined. And you will have to sell world rights so that the publishing industry can adequately exercise those e-book rights, making any money *you* would receive on foreign rights vanish.

If you have what I'm now beginning to believe is the standard agency rider in your contract, you will also lose a percentage of any auxiliary rights sale to that agent *even if you fired that agent* in the meantime and someone else negotiated the deal. Plus that agent will be entitled to a percentage of any work you write using that series, those characters, that world, or anything resembling that.

There is a line item in Albini's article at the end. Someone else made money on that album deal. It was the previous label ($50,000). Change the word "label" to "agent" and you start to see the scope of the problem here.

If you are a *New York Times* bestselling author, and you sign a traditional publishing contract with most modern terms, and you do so with an agent—and not an IP attorney—negotiating for you, lucky you. You have the *chance,* and I mean *chance,* of earning more than your advance. You'd better be a top-ten *New York Times* bestseller and you'd better stay on the list for longer than one week. Because all the things I said above will apply.

The only difference? You'll get a sizeable six-figure advance, and if you're smart, you'll write at least two books per year. Until the opportunities dwindle, and they will.

Do you know how many former *New York Times* bestsellers I'm friends with? Do you know how many of them can't get a traditional publishing deal for more than a five-figure advance?

Most of them.

If they're offered a deal at all.

Folks, all of the things you learned about agents, editors, and book publishers used to be true.

Ten years ago, you needed an agent to open the doors for you in traditional publishing.

Ten years ago, your editor—who loved books (and still loves books)—could go to bat for you within the publishing house and actually win the fight, protecting you, her author.

Ten years ago, traditional publishing—while not a friendly industry (I don't think there are any)—did not screw its artists the way that the music industry and Hollywood did.

Ten years ago.

Not any more.

Things have changed so rapidly that the contract I signed last September is not a contract I would sign today. Not because of the advance or even because of some of the contract terms. But because it's a *multi-book* contract. And honestly, y'all, I want to decide from book to book if I want a traditional publishing company to handle everything.

Sometimes I will. Sometimes I'll use a novel as a loss leader. Sometimes I will want the traditional publishing house to take all of the risk.

Sometimes.

But not all the time.

And certainly not for multiple books in the same series. Now, if that series isn't being well handled by my publisher, I want the option to do it myself. If the book is being well handled, I want to ask for a greater advance and better contract terms.

I have clout for the first time in my lovely little midlist career. I plan to use it.

Most of my friends and colleagues will slowly discover that they can no longer make a living as a writer. They'll wonder what happened. They'll wake up one day—after their latest multi-book contract is complete—and wonder what the hell happened.

They changed industries. They moved from a hidebound old-fashioned industry to a Hollywood-level shark pit—and they didn't even realize it happened.

It is happening as quickly, if not more quickly, than Robert Redford described with *All the President's Men*. Redford, savvy businessman that he is, saw the writing on the wall and decided to help save the kind of movies that he loved.

I am trying to save writers whose work I love. The only way to do that is to get them to realize that they have moved to a hostile and unforgiving world, one that is willing—no, eager—to take advantage of them.

The agents that they once trusted now answer to their agencies instead of to the writer. Those agencies are trying to steal a percentage of the writer's copyrights.

The editors whom they (rightfully) love have completely lost clout in their own industry and often can't keep the verbal promises that they make.

These writers need to learn business, and they need to learn it fast. Because the scammers have moved in, willing to take advantage of the writers who are unwilling to invest in themselves, unwilling to pay flat fees to companies that can do the work for them if they can't do the work themselves.

I'm sorry to tell you to stop trusting people. I know some of these people are your friends. Sadly, some of these people are my friends. In fact, many of these people are my friends.

And it breaks my heart, it really, really does.

But please, go look at that music industry link. Then realize that this is what's happening in publishing now.

If you want to do all the original work, create the content that everyone else is making a profit on, and get paid less than you would earn at 7/11, then don't learn any of this.

But if that idea scares you, if the idea that you might never earn more than your advance, and maybe not even all of that, then invest in yourself. Learn to say no.

And stop working on a business model that's ten years out of date.

Surviving the Transition

When I wrote "Writing Like It's 1999," I scared a lot of people. Many of them—most of them, judging by my private e-mail and the discussions I had in Los Angeles at a conference that following weekend—had no idea the industry had changed so much. Most of my conversations in Los Angeles, when I wasn't meeting with Hollywood people or doing my own business, were about that particular blog.

I want "Writing Like It's 1999" to scare you. I want to shock you awake, so that you understand what is happening to the industry that we all love. I want you to know that most of what you learned, experienced, and understand about the publishing industry—the industry you have worked in for decades—no longer applies.

Just as I expected, a small number of you hid your heads in the sand. One person even blogged that I had no idea what I was talking about because that writer's agent keeps that writer informed about changes in the publishing industry, and the agent says nothing of the sort is happening.

To that writer, and other writers like that writer, let me say, if your agent is giving you such silly advice, then I'd reassess your relationship with the agent. Because it sounds to me like you're doing the equivalent of taking advice about the financial industry from a pre-arrest Bernie Madoff.

There are still some excellent agents out there, and to a person, they all know how deeply and dangerously this world is changing. So, if your agent is telling you to stop worrying your pretty little head about this, you had better see that as a warning sign and reassess your relationship with that agent.

Most established writers, however, are terrified of the change and the rate of change. In the past, publishing has been a glacial industry. A change that would "sweep through" the industry would take about five years to make its "rapid" change.

Some of this change—particularly with the agents—has happened over the past ten years. But the most rapid change, in contracts, negotiations, rights deals, and the attitudes in the publishing houses themselves, has happened in the past two.

Why?

Let me give you a simple answer:

Traditional publishing has lost its monopoly. It used to control the distribution of books all over the United States and, indeed, all over the world. With the success of the e-reader and ease of electronic self-publishing, writers regained control over distribution.

Concurrent with that was the rise of a new model for print-on-demand. No longer does a writer have to purchase thousands of books at the cost of thousands of dollars. The writer can upload her novel at almost no out-of-pocket cost and not print a single copy until she has an order. In fact, the POD company, such as CreateSpace and LightningSource, will produce the book and ship it for the author, so there is no warehousing, no pile of books rotting in an author's basement.

In other words, all parts of the distribution chain are now available to the entrepreneurial author. Including audio books, since Audible has now instituted a system in which an author can do her own audio books.

Traditional publishers got blindsided by this. So did agents, who rely on their contacts in traditional publishing to make their living. And both groups are now in survival mode. They're trying to hang on to their hefty incomes in a new world they don't entirely understand

Mostly, they're doing so by making huge rights grabs from authors. Traditional publishers have more draconian contracts with a lot more clauses that they refuse to negotiate. Agents have decided to get as much ownership in their clients' property as they possibly can as well, mostly through putting up backlist as e-books, causing a huge conflict of interest. An agent who is also a publisher cannot adequately represent you to another publisher, because both the agent and that publisher are vying for your business—and the rights to your property.

I understand traditional publishing's reaction. I also understand why the agents are behaving the way they are. I also know that most longtime professional writers are extremely worried about this but aren't quite sure what to do.

So, let me give you some tips.

First, let's define some terms.

1. Indie Publishing: When I say indie publishing, I do *not* mean electronic publishing. I mean that the writer publishes her own writing on her own, either with the help of a flat-fee service or by doing all (or most) of the work herself. This writer, if she's smart, will produce both e-books and paper books and will learn how to market them to bookstores. Sounds daunting, doesn't it? But it isn't. It just takes time. More on this below.

2. Traditional publishing: Anything that uses the old model wherein a writer submits her work to a publisher, gets that work accepted or rejected, and if accepted, signs a contract. The publisher handles everything else from production to distribution.

3. Traditional agents: Agents who take a 15% commission on the books they sell to a traditional publisher. These agents *do not* publish anything. They operate in the old model, acting as their authors' advocates and looking out for their authors' interest. (And yes, there are still a handful of these agents out there.)

4. Agents/estributors: These people may have been traditional agents as recently as six months ago. Now, they will publish a writer's backlist for 15-50% of the net receipts. Many big-name agencies are moving to this model. Avoid at all costs.

5. Intellectual Property (IP) Attorneys: When I started in the business, there were only a handful of IP attorneys who handled publishing contracts. Now there are dozens of such attorneys all over the country. They know publishing contract language, charge an hourly fee, and will negotiate publishing contracts from every country in the world. Many of these attorneys also know how to handle Hollywood contracts, gaming contracts, and comic book contracts as well as most auxiliary rights contracts. You don't have to use the same attorney on every book. You can hire different attorneys for different things. I now recommend that writers get IP attorneys instead of agents.

6. Established writers: Writers who have published a lot of novels. These writers have survived on their writing income for at least a decade, maybe more. They may have published two novels, they may have published two hundred, but they have worked as a freelancer in this industry long enough to have survived some good times and some bad times. And let me say to those of you who are unpublished or not-very-well published, there are a lot more established writers out there than you've been led to believe. Each genre has hundreds of them.

So now that we all understand what I mean by my terminology, let's move on.

Most of the established writers are extremely worried about this transition. They're smart enough about business to understand that the change is here and that the change will have an impact on them. Established writers aren't as nimble as unpublished writers or newly published writers. Established writers have existing relationships, some decades-old, with publishing companies and with agents. Established writers have been doing things the same way ever since they came into the business. These writers may have hired and fired a few agents, may have had books orphaned or had to change their writing name a few times, but these writers know how to survive.

In the old world.

And they know just enough about this world to realize that they have a gigantic learning curve ahead of them. By learning curve, I do *not* mean that established writers must learn how to self-publish or indie publish. Established writers must learn the industry they're in all over again. Because everything they learned in the past ten, twenty, or thirty years no longer applies. Daunting, yes. Impossible, no.

Let me help.

Time

First, realize that you have a lot of time to learn this. I know, I know. Everyone from bloggers to your agent screams at you to make decisions now. Several established writers who blog believe that you must get your backlist up ASAP. Agents/estributors want you to give them your backlist to put up ASAP. Traditional publishers want to amend your existing contracts to give them more e-rights ASAP.

We'll deal with the bloggers in a minute.

Let me assist you with the agents/estributors and the traditional publishers. Whenever a person who has a financial interest in you or your work pressures you to make a decision quickly, that person wants you to make a deal that is not in your best interest. This applies to everything from buying a car to amending your publishing contract. Guaranteed, if you make a new deal or amend an old deal on a *hurry-up, hurry-up* timeline, that deal will not benefit you.

Breathe. Consult friends/experts and our new friend, the IP attorney. Do not make any of these decisions lightly.

Almost every amended contract clause I have seen in the past six months has been a bad deal for the writer. Compare that clause to the clause in your contract. Make sure the new clause is better, and not just in one aspect, but in all aspects.

For example, an amendment I saw recently seemed better until you got to the last paragraph. There it said that the writer was not entitled to a deal that a writer of different stature received. "Different stature" was not defined. Even if it was, the clause still smelled. It definitely meant that the midlist writer couldn't get bestseller terms. But it might also have meant that writer A couldn't get the same terms as writer B even though both of them had sold 10,000 copies of their latest novel and both of them were working in the same genre.

That clause only benefits the publisher, by giving the publisher the ability to turn down any change in the contract by saying it does not apply.

See why you need to take time with these things?

Say no. A lot.

Research everything before you make a decision, and make it in your own time. Do what's best for you, not what's best for the writer down the street. Make sure you can live with your decision in all cases—if your book is successful, and if it fails. Because some clauses only kick in when a book has success. And others ensure that you can't get your rights back if a book fails.

Many of you established writers don't have any out-of-print books. This means that you won't have to make any decisions in the new publishing world until it comes time to sign a new contract. That might be six months from now or two years from now. Fulfill your contract, but as you do so, keep a jaundiced eye on two things: first, on the changes in contractual language that other writers are dealing with; and secondly, on what is happening with your agent and your agency.

If your agent is moving from the traditional model to the estributor model, decide if you want to remain with someone who has such a serious conflict of interest. Also make sure that your traditional agent will be in business two years from now. Many traditional agents—ethical down to their core—have realized that they don't like the changes in the industry and are leaving it. Don't find yourself in the position of looking for a new agent when your contract is up for renewal. Talk to your agent and figure out what is happening with his business over the next few years. Keep that dialogue open.

Finally, let's deal with this pressure to put your entire backlist up now. If you have no out-of-print books and you've been in this business for ten to twenty years, then many of your previously published books will not have an e-rights clause. Your publisher will know that and will try to get the e-rights from you. Think hard about what's in your best interest before you sign amendments granting your publisher e-rights.

You might be better off retaining those e-rights for yourself and indie publishing those books. Or finding someone else to indie publish them for you. Before you give those rights to your agent/estributor, however, research other methods of publishing them. I will deal with this aspect in-depth below.

Finally, let me add one more thing about amendments. I recently got an e-rights amendment to my contract from one of my publishers. The amendment had two clauses. The first clause reiterated what was already in my contract.

The second clause gave the publisher the right to adapt, amend, enhance, abridge, and alter my book so that it could be used in any technology that exists or might be developed, including, but not limited to, smart-phone technology, video, sound, and imagery. This clause would allow my traditional publisher to tamper with my book in any way that the publisher saw fit. It also gave them a backwards way to make my book into a movie or a television show.

I wrote the publisher a curt letter saying I would not sign the amendment. The publisher wrote back and promised *in the e-mail* not to exercise any of the rights that bothered me. But the publisher would not remove the language from the amendment.

For those of you who do not understand contract law: the publisher's promise means nothing. Only the wording of that amendment will apply in any dispute I might have with the publisher. Unless the publisher is willing to change clause two of the amendment, I will not sign it. And here's the thing most writers do not understand: *I have no legal obligation to sign it.* Just because the publisher wants me to sign that amendment doesn't mean I have to. I can say—and am saying—no.

For the rest of you, those who have an out-of-print backlist, you do not have to publish it tomorrow. In fact, it would be hard to get your entire backlist up tomorrow.

The reason so many agents/estributors are getting established writers to sign with them is that established writers believe a brand-new myth, promulgated by bloggers. That myth states that you *must* get your backlist up now or miss the gravy train.

No. Not true. Readers who want your backlist now will want your backlist two years from now.

Take the time to make a decision that is right for you.

I consistently recommend that established writers do *not* pay a commission to someone to get their backlist up in e-book. The writer will lose a tremendous amount of money over time. But most established writers don't have enough money to pay a flat fee for every backlist novel they have. Let's use my backlist. As of last summer, I had 30 novels that were not in print. If I spent a $1000 flat fee per novel to get them all up last August, I would have had to have $30,000 to do so.

I didn't have $30,000 to spare last August. I'm sure most of you don't either. This is why most writers have signed up with estributors who take a percentage, so that they won't have to pay money up front.

But if you don't hurry, if you take 30 months or 60 months or 90 months to get those books up, you'll still make money on your backlist. You'll retain all of your rights, and you'll eventually make money—a lot more money than you will if you trust an agent/estributor. These people are unregulated and do not have the accounting systems in place to deal with the problems that are coming down the road. This percentage/commission system is ripe for embezzlement.

Many of you can afford $1000 per month to get your backlist up. Many of you can afford $500 or $250 or $125 per month to get the list up. Figure out what you can spend, then save that money until you can afford to hire a flat-fee service. Put up one book at a time. Realize that you're not losing anything by waiting and are, in fact, gaining control over your work.

Time is on your side. Don't be pressured into making any decisions, no matter what your friends are doing, what your agent says, or what your publisher wants. Make the decision that's right for you.

And please, do whatever you can to keep control over your career. You need to learn this new business. Take the time to do so.

Just remember: it took you years to learn the business the first time. It'll take you at least six months to learn this new business. Don't panic. You can do it, and if you do, you'll be much better off.

Because the changes in the industry benefit the writer who is willing to learn the business. We are gaining control over our own work and our own careers. Please don't let anyone steal that control from you. Understand what you sign, learn how the changes in the industry will impact you, and remember: you have all the time in the world.

Publishers

Many established writers are happy with their current publishers. Some established writers have never had a work go out of print or orphaned. A few haven't had any problems with traditional publishing at all and see no reason to abandon a system that has worked for them for decades.

Personally, I think established writers whose traditional publishers are doing a good job for them would be silly to abandon that route for a route the writer might not be suited for. The established writer can use short stories or collections or unpublished works under a pen name to try the indie publishing route. (And please remember, by indie publishing I do *not* mean electronic publishing; I also include print publishing in that.)

However, publishing has changed—and changed dramatically—in the past two years.

So what's a traditionally published, established writer to do in this changing world? How can she protect her livelihood if she doesn't want to venture out on her own or abandon her publisher? What if she's a bestseller, perhaps, who is benefiting from the publisher's promotion and ability to get tens of thousands of books into airports and other non-book venues all at the same time? Should this writer ignore the changes?

No.

This writer, more than any other writer, is in danger of losing money and copyrights, of, in fact, going from making a lot of money to making little or no money at all. How can she lose money when she will probably maintain her bestseller status, her sales will probably go up, and her work will go into more markets than ever before?

Simple. Her contract terms will change and she might not even notice.

Amazon announced in May of 2011 that it now sells more e-books than print books. This announcement makes sense for two reasons: 1) Amazon is a mail-order company, and it's more convenient to order books electronically than it is to have them shipped (and it's cheaper as well); and 2) Amazon's e-reader currently dominates the market. It'll be greater news when Barnes & Noble makes the same announcement.

But the relevant part of that news to the established writer happy with her traditional publisher is this: by the time the writer's two- or three-book contract comes up for renewal, e-books will probably comprise 50% of the market. And while the writer's contract terms for print books—especially if she's a bestseller—are very good, her contract terms for e-books will have gotten worse.

We will discuss legal terms in this section. Please remember that I am not a lawyer and am only stating opinions here. Informed opinions, yes, but not *legal* opinions. Got that? Okay.

Ten years ago, my midlist contract gave me 50% of the retail price for every e-book sold. Now, my contracts with traditional publishers give me 25% of the net price for every e-book sold. The different is significant, and it's more than the 25% loss it initially looks like. As J. Daniel Sawyer points out in "Principles of Contracts: Nothing But Net" on the meaning of the word "net" in contracts, "net" usually means nothing at all. (You can find Dan's post at jdsawyer.net.)

So far, publishing has avoided Hollywood-level accounting practices, in which anyone who signs a contract for the percentage of the net *and believes he will get any money from that clause* is a fool. Gaming companies do the same thing. They do a lot of creative accounting to make certain that there is no net—or, at least, no net profit.

Right now, publishing contracts do not include the word "profit" in their net promise. Right now, the contracts *imply* that the writer will get 25% of the net receipts that the publisher gets from the distributor (say Amazon). But many contracts do not explicitly state that.

So, the established writer's first task in renegotiating her contract is to make certain her e-rights pay her as well as her print rights do. That means she'll have to do some hardcore negotiation. We'll talk about negotiation a little farther down. (And if you want an in-depth piece on negotiation, I discuss it in my short book *How To Negotiate Anything* and also in my *Freelancer's Survival Guide*.)

The writer should do her best to get a percentage of the book's retail price. The retail price is a *fixed* price, from which everything else flows. Even if the publisher only receives payment for half of the retail price, the author should receive a royalty rate on the retail price.

Publishers have eaten away at this standard even in print contract deals with discount schedules built into the contract. But the discount schedule works off the retail price. (For books priced at 50% of retail, the author will receive x royalty, is often how the discount schedule wording begins.) Fight for that in the royalty rates for e-books as well.

Right now, no one seems to be arguing for this, instead trying to tinker with the rates offered by the publisher. One solution I've seen, which I seriously dislike, is this: the publisher offers to renegotiate the royalty rate every three years, to bring the rate in line with "industry standard."

In the contracts I've seen that make this offer, "industry standard" is defined this way: "industry standard as used herein shall mean the royalty rate … that is routinely paid by at least two major publishers (such as Random House, Harper/

Morrow…) to authors whose stature is similar to that of" the writer involved in this deal.

There are several problems with "industry standard" defined this way, the first being this: In the past ten years, "industry standard" as so defined (meaning what was offered by other "major publishers") has declined. It used to be 50% of the retail price. It is no longer. In other words, you could ask for the current industry standard and get a much worse deal. So, that part of this clause is a double-edged sword.

But as I mentioned previously, the part I really don't like is the "to authors whose stature is similar" to that of the writer in question. An undefined term, such as "stature," means nothing. I might have equivalent book sales to another writer, but she might have won more awards or is the current Hot Young Thing, and a publisher could claim that our stature is not similar. And how would I argue this? In court?

These kinds of clauses, which look great at first glance, are actually much more harmful to the writer than the old-fashioned percentage of the retail price. This is simply a way of making a writer feel like she has control, when, in effect, she is giving up control.

Another clause to beware of in the e-rights clause of your new contract is this one:

"The Author hereby grants to the Publisher…the exclusive license to produce, publish, sell, distribute and further license any Electronic Version of the Work…. 'Electronic Version' means versions that include the Work… in a *complete, condensed, adapted, or abridged version* and in *compilations for performance and display in any manner whether sequentially or non-sequentially* and together with accompanying sounds and images, if any, transmissible by *any* electronic means, method or device *(including but not limited to* electronic and machine-readable *media* and online or satellite-based transmission *or any other device or medium for electronic reproduction or transmission whether now or hereafter known or developed…*)" [Emphasis mine.]

Yikes! Ick! No. Never, ever, ever, ever sign this clause. Think about this: movies are digitized—they are performance, and they are often distributed online. Not only does that clause allow someone to monkey with your work, abridging it, taking it out of order, *adding things to it*, making it into a performance piece, adding sound effects, but it also is a backwards way of granting television rights, video display rights, and any other *performance* right, so long as that performance can be distributed electronically.

And don't believe that someone in your publishing house won't use that clause down the road. The editor you trust may leave, the publishing company might change hands, and a clause that was designed for one thing will be used for something completely different.

Remember, I'm not a lawyer. This is not legal advice. But *in my opinion*, this clause is one of the most harmful to appear in the last year. Sign at your own peril.

What you want to grant to your publisher is this: "Electronic book rights," which should be defined as "the unenhanced verbatim text of the work." And that's *it*. Nothing else. Not anything yet to be developed, not any performance rights. Nothing more.

Got that?

This is all very, very, very important, because we're going to assume that your books will remain in print for the next decade. Which means that you will not get the rights back to them. Which means that the clauses you sign now might be exercised five years from now, and if you sign a clause that gives you (in effect) 25% of net, and your publisher moves to creative Hollywood accounting and there is no net, and then e-book sales rise to 75% of the market—well, then, that cushy living you're making on your royalties *will* evaporate. Notice I didn't say *might*. I said *will*.

Contracts are super important right now.

You must also want your out-of-print clause to be extremely tight. I recommend that you only license your e-rights for a set time period—five years, ten, it doesn't matter. At that point, you renegotiate the contract terms. And that replaces your out-of-print clause. It's the only way to hang on to some rights.

What most publishers use is what I call "a speed limit": In the past, I've argued that you have a speed limit—if the book doesn't sell 300 copies in that time period (in any format) or if the book is not available for sale at all. But those are old-fashioned ways of thinking. Better to have a limit on the rights. If the publisher refuses, then you can decide to walk or not. If you chose to stay, make sure that the word "sell" does not include any books given away for free. Because a publisher could easily make those 300 copies with a one-day free promotion offer.

Make sure that a print-on-demand version of your book does not count as "in print." Nor should any second-party books count as in print. Meaning if the book was licensed to another company to produce the audio because you licensed audio rights to your original publisher, and the audio version is still in print but no version from your original publisher is in print, then that book should be counted as out of print. Only the actions by your original publisher should count toward in print.

Watch out for your option clause. Try to avoid signing one at all. In the past, option clauses were like job security, but no longer. Option clauses have now become a way to tie a writer to a publishing house and to prevent her from working for anyone else. So, strike your option clause if possible.

If it's not possible, limit the option to the next book in this particular series, under this particular name (or pen name). If the book isn't in a series, then limit by genre. The next contemporary political thriller under Pen Name (or your Author Name—not your legal name). Give the publisher 30 days from the turn-in of your proposal to exercise the option, and nothing else.

Watch your warranty clause. Now, many publishers are reverting to an old practice. They want writers to warrant that the writer will not write *anything* until this particular book under this particular contract is *published.*

This used to be a separate clause, and very easy to find. It existed in a lot of contracts 20 years ago then faded away.

Now, it's back with a vengeance. It used to be that the writer guaranteed the book she had just contracted for would be her next book and no other book would compete against it.

Now, she's guaranteeing that she will not *write* another book until this one is published. And in many cases, the publisher enjoins her from writing *anything*.

This clause, which has been in every new book contract I have seen from traditional New York publishers in the past six months, is buried in the warranties. Which are the boilerplate part of the contract, the part that includes bankruptcies and acts of God. A lot of established writers stopped reading the legal gobbledygook in the boilerplate years ago, and have been snared by this clause.

Don't you be one of them.

I can go on and on and on about contract clauses to avoid. Those are some of the big ones. When you get your new contract, compare it to your previous contracts. I'd even go back a few—maybe back to your contracts from the late 1990s—and try to reinstate those terms.

If you find a one-word change in your new contract, and you don't understand why that word is there, find out. If the word has been changed, that word is important. And you can bet all the changes will benefit the publisher.

So…

You find these clauses in your new contract. What do you do?

Before you do anything, figure out what you can live with and what you can't live with. Figure out what's important to you in this contract and what isn't.

Recently, I refused to sign a contract for a short piece that allowed the publisher to make any editorial change they deemed necessary. Which meant that they could rewrite the entire thing, change everything about the piece itself, and still publish it under my name.

If I can't get clauses like that changed, I walk. I've walked from clauses like that for thirty years, including on one of the very first non-fiction contracts I was supposed to sign.

No one changes my words without my permission—and I don't give blanket permission. Period.

Yet I may take a book contract with percentage of net price because I might not be looking at that book as a moneymaker for me. I might look at it as a way to reach new readers. I've taken flat fees on projects in the past. But I knew what I was signing. I knew the risks I was taking, and I was willing to take those risks.

So, pick where your battles will be, then fight them. Figure out when you will retreat, what you will compromise on, and what you will fight to the death for.

And if you plan to fight to the death, then that means you might have to walk. Against the advice of your agent, against extra money your publisher might throw at you, against a guaranteed publishing deal.

When you say no to a clause, mean no.

I have walked from dozens of contracts long before publishing's monopoly on distribution was broken, and without exception, I eventually found another publisher and usually a better deal.

The keyword here? *Eventually*. I couldn't always turn the project around and sell it elsewhere quickly. But I would sell it down the road.

And watch out for someone who will tell you that refusing this deal, turning down these contract terms, will ruin your career. Naw. Let me tell you there is only one way to ruin your career—and it isn't by standing up for yourself. It's by giving up writing altogether.

Someone who tries to pressure you into a deal with threats or with intimidation, by speeding you along or by telling you that you will destroy your career, doesn't have your best interest at heart. That person has another agenda.

If you want to stick with your traditional publisher, then make sure that your contracts benefit you and will continue to benefit you in the future. Negotiate. Think ahead. Make sure that you understand what the contract in front of you says.

If you don't understand, then ask for help—not just from your agent or an IP attorney, but other writers who've been in the same position. Get multiple opinions.

Never accept a promise that clauses in the contract will not get exercised. If those clauses are in the contract, then assume someday someone will put that clause into effect.

And double-check. Make sure a clause that might benefit you if the book sells poorly doesn't hurt you if the book sells well. Because a lot of contract clauses actually *decrease* the amount of money you will receive if a book succeeds.

Finally, do not expect your agent to negotiate a good deal for you. You might have the most reputable agent in the world, but that agent doesn't know what's best for you. More and more I've been talking to agent friends of mine and discovering that they do not understand the changes that are happening in publishing. So, these agents can't protect you from those changes because the agents have no idea what the pitfalls might be.

If you hire an intellectual property attorney to negotiate for you instead of an agent (which is what I now recommend), that attorney will do his best, but he will only do what you tell him to do. If you fail to tell him to check the warranty clause, then he won't negotiate that horrible write-only-for-this-publisher clause out of your contract.

Writers have always been in charge of their own careers, but in the past most established writers trusted their editors, publishers, and agents to work with them and not against them. These writers knew enough not to trust a Hollywood contract but would sign a book contract after only scanning it.

Those days are gone. If you do that now—even if you're a successful *New York Times* bestseller—you might lose every single dollar you make. You must negotiate your own contract and get the very best terms you can.

Your livelihood depends on it.

Will you get all of the changes you want? Of course not. You'll have to compromise on most things. But don't be the only one to compromise. Your publisher must compromise, as well.

Be clear with your publisher: You want to continue working with them. But you also want to continue to make a very good living in this new world of publishing. If your current publisher can't modify the new terms of their contract, then you might have to look for a new publisher.

Be prepared for that.

Be prepared to defend your work and your livelihood.

The best place to do that—in a traditional publishing environment—is with the contracts you sign. Make sure they're the very best they can be.

For you.

Agents

I had a dream, as recently as six months ago, that agents would help writers through this transition in publishing. I believed that agents would band together and fight to the death for the best possible terms in a contract for every writer.

If agents had done that, the e-rights clauses I talked about above wouldn't be in contracts. If agents had been willing to convince their clients to walk from certain book deals, we would all be benefiting from new and improved contracts from traditional publishers.

Silly me. I was thinking about agents as something that, perhaps, they never were. I wasn't thinking about their business model, but my own.

Agents are a relatively new phenomenon in publishing. Agents became important in the 1940s and 1950s when New York City became too expensive for the average writer to live in. Before that, writers had to live in or near New York to thrive in the publishing marketplace. The writers actually had to go to the publishers' offices themselves.

When writers moved to far-flung places, like Des Moines or Seattle, the writers needed an advocate, someone to contact the publisher for them. Agents stepped in, and acted as the writer's representative in exchange for 10% of each sale that the agent made.

Agents have always had a slightly shady reputation. If you look at the movies of the 1930s and 1940s, you'll see theatrical agents portrayed as sleazy and barely tolerable types. In the movie *Frost/Nixon*, there's a lovely scene in which Richard Nixon takes on the most famous literary agent of them all, Swifty Lazar, and wins. Nixon treated Lazar the way that most people treated agents in those days, as a necessary evil.

When publishing had a monopoly and business was conducted by telephone, lunch meetings, and the postal service, it was easy for an agent to make his name on his access to the publishing world. A lot of agents, like the famous Swifty, had more access than any writer could ever dream of having.

Agents, in those days, were salesmen, hustlers, trying to sell as many projects as many times as possible. Because agents at that time were more like real estate agents. The literary agent didn't have a "relationship" with their client. The agent had a product to hawk—a single book—and the agent had to sell that. If he didn't, or if he didn't do a very good job on the sale, then the writer went to another agent or did the work himself.

By the mid-1980s, however, this agent model was fading. The boutique agency, where a handful of agents banded together to rent office space, became the thing. Some of this, again, happened because of the cost of doing business in New York. It became too expensive for the average agent to have his own office.

But the agents also learned that by banding together, they could act on behalf of all of their clients, expanding their clout. So now, Agent #1 wasn't representing 3 bestsellers. Instead, Number One Agency was representing 15 bestsellers, and by gum, Really Big Publishing House should acknowledge that by giving Number One Agency good contract terms.

This change was happening when I came into the business, and clearly I imprinted on it. At this time, also, agents started charging 15% instead of 10% and some places began having their writers sign agency agreements that stated that the agent would represent the client (not the work) until either party terminated the agreement.

Those agency agreements weren't that big a deal. They were breakable with a single phone call, and there would be no hard feelings. Also about this time, publishers realized they had a liability issue when they gave a writer's check to the agent. So, publishers requested an agency clause in the contract of any writer whose agent got the check first. All that clause would say was that the writer authorized Really Big Publishing House to issue the writer's checks to Number One

Agency, and that would be considered payment under terms of the contract.

Again, no big deal. It covered the publisher's ass in case Number One Agency ran off with the writer's funds (as some agents did). Without that clause, the publisher would have had to either issue another check to the writer or get sued for breach of contract.

Another ten years passed. Boutique agencies grew into major corporations, and those corporations realized they should branch out into Hollywood. Things work differently in Hollywood. Contracts are draconian things that take money from the creative artist and give all of that money to hangers-on, if the creative artist isn't careful.

At the turn of the century, Hollywood business practices infected the boutique and corporate literary agencies. I have examples in my files from one former boutique agency (now a corporate agency) showing the evolution of the agent clause they put in a publishing contract. It went from "send the check here" to this [emphasis mine]:

"The Author hereby *irrevocably* appoints [Agency]…to act in *all matters* pertaining to or arising out of this agreement and *all other agreements, licensing, or otherwise dispersing of any rights in the Work in any form or media, and including any works for which there are options under this agreement…* In consideration for services rendered, the Author *irrevocably* assigns and transfers to the Agent a sum equal to 15% of all monies due the Author under this Agreement and *related agreements….*"

It ends with this rather astonishing sentence: *The provisions of this paragraph shall survive the termination of this Agreement.*

Um, excuse me? Lawyers out there, tell me how this is possible.

That paragraph is a minefield of horribleness. It *irrevocably* assigns at least 15% of earnings from the sale of any rights in the book to the agent, as well as the same amount in works that are covered under the option clause. So, if the agent negotiates a broad option like this one: "The publishing house has the option on the author's next work," then the agent will earn his 15% in whatever that next work is…even if the publishing contract is terminated.

(Yeah, I know. I just said that last sentence probably isn't valid. But what do I know? I'm not a lawyer. And besides, do you want to be the poor sap who has to spend years in court proving that particular clause is invalid?)

That agency clause is nowhere near the worst I've seen in the past few months. Writers have been sharing some real doozies with me from corporate agencies.

Here's the next big offender:

This agent clause, which goes into a publishing agreement, has all the traditional stuff about payment. And then it says [again, emphasis mine], "For services rendered and *about to be rendered,* the Author does hereby *irrevocably* assign and *transfer* to said agent and said agent shall retain, a sum equal to 15% *as an agency coupled with an interest....*"

Oh, my God. I wouldn't have signed that as a twenty-one year old newly birthed nonfiction writer. It sounds scary because it is. It means that the writer has assigned his agent—irrevocably—15% of the book. "An interest" is a legal term and it means that the agent now has a piece of that property: 15%-worth to be exact.

We'll talk about the implications of this in a minute.

But let's now move to the worst offender I've seen in the past few months. I'm not going to say it is the worst offender out there, because I haven't seen all of them. It's just the worst of my little trio of horrors.

This big name agency has the same clause as the one above. But coupled with the agency agreement—a five-page document that gives the agency the right to negotiate for the writer on any matters on the writer's behalf. It also gives the agency "commissions earned by, paid to or credited to" the Author "or any entity owned by or controlled by" the Author "in perpetuity."

Seriously. In perpetuity.

And in case the writer missed that point, there's this: "The Author understands and agrees that the provisions of this Agreement which by their very nature survive the expiration of the Term of this Agreement." And then it goes on to list all the negotiation, money clauses, and interest in the work clauses as surviving the Term of the Agreement.

In other words, you can fire this agency, but you—and your heirs, and any corporation that you form or trust that you create—will owe that agency money *forever*.

Now, technically, forever isn't an acceptable contract term. Contracts need an end date to be valid. But again, do you (or your kids or your grandkids) want to be the one to go to court to win that fight?

This five-page agent agreement is so egregious, by the way, that even if you fire the agency, they can still negotiate a deal for you and undercut any new deal you might negotiate for yourself. And you, if you signed this agreement, gave them permission to do so.

I read this thing and wanted to go screaming into the night. Because I know dozens of people who have signed it.

(Okay, Kris. Breathe. Breathe.)

So, let's look at the implications of all this stuff, in relation to our agent history lesson, above.

These egregious clauses started showing up in book contracts and agency agreements around the turn of this century. Big agencies had become the norm, and they worked on the Hollywood model.

It's clear from these clauses that the important entity in these agreements isn't the author. It's the agency. In the case of two of these clauses, the agency is making an actual rights grab on an author's work—*and the authors who signed this stuff allowed that rights grab*, probably without understanding what they were signing.

Here's how it works in practice. Author A gets pissed at Number One Agency and wants to hire The Grass Is Greener Agency. The Grass Is Greener Agency sells Author A's next book, and the day after the sale is announced, The Grass Is

Greener Agency gets a phone call from Number One Agency that says, "You didn't have the right to sell that book (see egregious clause #2). But you did, so give us our percentage."

Author A has a choice: either go to court or pay a 30% commission on the new book (15% to the new agent, and 15% to the old one). Court will take years and Author A could lose the case. The 30% is the best option here. And that 30% will continue on all projects related to that book, and maybe on all future projects.

An even worse case? That last agreement, in which The Grass Is Greener Agency gets the phone call informing them that they had no right to make this deal and the deal is invalid because Number One Agency negotiated a different deal on the author's behalf with a different publishing house. Author A, after all, had signed away the rights to negotiate for himself in that horrible five-page agent agreement.

You think things like this don't happen? In the past month, I've heard two separate stories of big deals gone awry because of this very thing.

And let me give you a parenthetical scare: if you signed some of those egregious agent clauses, you might owe your agent 15% of that book, even if it's out of print from its original publisher, *even if you e-publish the book yourself.* You gave your very smart agent 15% of your property. Just sayin'.

So, let's back up to the beginning of this section. My own little dream that agents would defend writers against publishers.

What the hell was I thinking?

I was operating not like it was 1999, but like it was 1989. And I was believing the myth of agent as author advocate. Agents have always been in this game for themselves.

Don't believe me? Then look at this little parenthetical aside about the Scott Meredith Literary Agency from the great Lawrence Block in *Mystery Scene Magazine* #118. In a column about Evan Hunter, Block writes about the porn fiction market of the late 1950s (and stresses that what was called "porn" back then is what we call "erotica" now).

"The foremost publisher of this erotica," he writes, "was Bill Hamling, whose imprints included Nightstand Books and Midnight Reader, and Scott Meredith had an exclusive deal to feed Hamling a steady supply of manuscripts. (Scott got 10% of what his writers were paid, of course, and we've since learned that he also got a packaging fee of $1000 a book. So, when I wrote a book for $1000, I received $900 and my agent pocketed $1100. What a guy!)"

See why my dream was silly? Most agents have always been in this business to act in their own best interests. I say "most" because I do know a few agents who are really ethical folk, who are really trying to do the best by their authors, who really believe that they are the authors' advocates. If you have an agent like that, count yourself lucky.

Before you pat yourself on the back, however, check your agency clause in your most recent publishing contract. If it looks like any of the above, you have trouble. Your agent might be ethical, but he might work for a big corporate agency that isn't ethical at all. And the agency is named in that clause, not your individual agent.

Checking your agency clause in your most recent publishing contract is the best way to see who your agent is working for—himself or you. If any of the egregious clauses I mentioned above are in the agency clause of your latest publishing contract, your agent does not work for you. He works for the agency.

The second way to see whom your agent is working for is to look at your agency agreement. If you have one that lasts past that phone call in which you want to terminate (without cause) your "relationship" with your agent, then your agent doesn't work for you. He works for himself or his agency.

Really, honestly, truthfully, if you signed an agency agreement at all—even if it's a simple one—your agent probably doesn't work for you. The best agents still work on a handshake and don't put an agency clause in your publishing contract past the instructions on dispersal of funds. And yes, there are a few who still work that way. (And no, I won't tell you who they are for two reasons: 1) They don't want to get inundated; and 2) I haven't worked with most of them, so I only know about them through friends. In fact, some of them are friends. So don't e-mail me and ask.)

The biggest red flag that your agent doesn't give a damn about you is a really simple one: Your agent has started an e-publishing business for all of his clients' backlists.

The agent who starts an e-publishing business is no longer an agent. He's a publisher. And he is now competition with publishers out there. I'm not the only one who sees it that way. Publishers are complaining about it, too.

Let me tell you two separate stories, both true.

1. A friend of mine has a bestselling series with a well-known traditional publisher. Her agent has recently started a backlist e-publishing company. The friend got an offer from her traditional publisher for the same terms as her previous books. That includes e-rights.

The agent tried to negotiate away the e-rights, and when that didn't happen, stalled the negotiation, refusing to budge on these terms. The author had no idea what was going on until she was talking to her editor on the phone. The editor asked what was going on and told the writer about the stalled negotiation.

Until this point, the author had thought the stall was coming from the publisher. In fact, that was what the agent had told this author.

I wish I could tell you that the author fired the agent and continued the negotiations on her own. She didn't. But she forced the issue, at least, and the traditional publisher has the e-rights just like in the previous contracts.

I also wish I could tell you this is an isolated case, but I have heard this story in different forms from about six writers now, some of whom had something similar happen to them and some of whom were screaming at their writer friends in the same situation to fire the damn agent now. This isn't just one agent, by the way, but several—all of whom are now e-publishers.

2. A major agent is offering to buy the backlist of old-time writers, many of whom no longer have books in print, for a flat fee of $25,000. A publisher recently offered an advance and royalties for one of these writer's backlists, *and the agent refused to present the deal to the writer, whom the agent theoretically represented.*

This, too, is happening a lot. To an impoverished writer, $25,000 seems like a lot of money for something that's in a drawer gathering dust. But if the writer puts the backlist up himself, he'll make more than that over time. And even if that writer doesn't listen to sensible old me and do it himself, and instead hires an estributor for 15% of the take to put up the backlist, that writer would still make more money than if he sold his backlist for that flat $25,000.

So…

You look at your contract and see an egregious agency clause. You realize you signed a bad agent agreement. Or you discover that your agent has set himself up as an e-publisher.

What do you do?

In cases one and two, you'd better figure out what you signed and what it means before you take any action at all. I'd hire an IP attorney and ask him to vet your contracts and documents so you know what your risks and liabilities are before you take action.

Then, take action. The action might be as simple as never ever ever allowing that agency clause in your publishing contract again. Or it might require you to get rid of that particular agent. If you do get rid of the agent, do not jump back into the frying pan with another agent. Don't sign an agency agreement, and don't agree to any more of those horrible clauses.

If your agent has become an e-publisher, fire that agent now. That agent is not working in your best interest and never will again (if they ever did). Your agent has left the agenting business and has become a publisher, so your agent now has a conflict of interest.

If you feel you need an agent, find one who does not do e-publishing. And don't sign an agency agreement.

Earlier, I mentioned the agent's business model. Here's the key point: with publishing changing, the old 10-15% of each sale will not give an agent enough money to continue running his business—unless all of his clients are bestsellers. (This is why so many agents started chasing that bestseller-only dream a few years back.)

Agents are smart about business. They saw the handwriting on the wall before publishers and writers did. However, agents have no idea how to thrive in this new environment. Their old business model doesn't work, and if a writer indie or self-publishes, then the agent can't get a percentage of that, either.

Agents, more than anyone else in publishing, are running scared. That's why they're trying to get ownership in a writer's property. That's why some are calling themselves "managers" now. That's why so many agents are experimenting with their business model.

Some agents see e-publishing as the only way to keep their own business alive. *You don't have to support their new business*. You have your own business to run.

Right now, while all of publishing is in flux, I'm advising new writers to avoid agents. Down the road, once the agents have a good business model again, my advice may change.

Things are dicier for the established writer. Established writers are used to having agents and for some reason are unwilling to learn how to do business without those agents.

(Let me give you a hint, folks. Most foreign deals come because someone got their hands on a book—not through an agent, but through a bookstore. Then, the foreign publisher contacts the U.S publisher and asks who has the foreign rights. That publisher can as easily point to the writer as to the writer's agent. The same goes for Hollywood. It's that simple. There's a thing called the Internet now. The world has gotten small. As long as you have a static website with a contact button, anyone—including a foreign publisher—can find you.)

So, established writer, your agent has become an e-publisher. You have fired that agent. What do you do now? I give you the same advice I give to new writers. Wait before you hire a new agent. Give the industry time to settle into its new pattern.

During the next two years, if you have a book deal to negotiate, hire an IP attorney. If you're like most established writers, you probably have a book deal that will take you through these next two years. You won't have to negotiate anything.

So, stay put, watch the trends, and make your decision when the time comes. If your agent has become a publisher, fire him at your leisure. Have a plan before you let that agent go.

Oh — and one other thing. These clauses I'm citing come from very reputable, established agencies. When I first red-flagged them several months ago, many of my established writer friends said they hadn't signed an agency agreement. These writers have been with their big reputable agencies since the 1980s, before this practice became common.

If you're one of those writers, find out what your agency's practice is with new clients. If some of your friends have signed on, ask if they had to sign an agency agreement. Ask to see that agreement.

If you're with one of these agencies, you'll be shocked.

I would advise you to leave any agency that has an agreement like that *even if you never signed one*. Why? Because that's the way the agency operates now. It doesn't operate in the client's interest; it operates in the agency's interest.

(I ran into this almost a decade ago as my once-good literary agency changed. I asked my agent to overnight a check. I live in the boonies, and I don't want checks greater than $1000 to sit in my mailbox down the hill and out of sight of my house. I wanted checks of that size or greater to come through a tracking service like Fed Ex that hand me the package directly. My then-agent said, "It's no longer company policy to send checks smaller than $10,000 through a private service." I said, "I'm the client. You work for me." My then-agent said, "Um, sorry. But I'm afraid I still can't do that." *And didn't budge*.

(Guess what happened to my relationship with that agent? Well, we're still friends…but we don't do business any longer. Not because of the agent. But because of changes in the *agency*.)

Your agent has to work for you. If any of the red flags I listed above apply to your agent now (not to the person that agent was five years ago), then you need to part ways with that agent before you negotiate another book contract. Many of you have years to make that decision. Many of you need to make that decision now.

But be cautious about what you jump to. Every agent I know is in flux. One of the best said to me a few months ago that he was considering retirement; he doesn't recognize the industry any longer and sees no place for himself in it. I wouldn't be surprised if several of the ethical agents go that route.

Time to start the research. Time to figure out if you're going to continue working with an agent or if you're going to hire an IP attorney to negotiate contracts for you. I recommend the IP attorney, but I am not you and I don't know your circumstances.

Be warned, however, that this business is changing—and the agency business model that existed since the 1950s is effectively gone. Don't keep your agent because you've always had an agent.

Be proactive. Figure out what's best for you—even if you end up with the status quo. Do the research, and be informed.

Otherwise, you might end up losing a 15% (or higher!) interest in your book because you blindly signed a contract that you didn't understand or because you made an agreement with someone you thought was trustworthy who is trustworthy no longer.

Good luck.

Plan for the Future

If you're one of those lucky writers with a number of existing book deadlines, then you have the time to figure out what you want to do with the rest of your career. You need to educate yourself on the changes in the industry as they pertain to you, from contract terms to the changes in agents to the way that royalties are now being paid.

Take the time. Look at these next few months or years until your deadlines are up as graduate school. Do homework every week on the changes in the industry, so when the time comes for you to make a choice as to what direction your career will take in the future, you will make an informed choice.

One of the biggest parts of your future will concern the way you receive your writing income and how you manage that income. Most established writers don't have a day job. We make our living off our writing. We get lump sums every six months or a year, and we make those sums last. If we're really lucky, we get royalties off our books, as well, although most book contracts are now structured so that the advance is in line with the number of copies that a book sells. The midlist writer almost never runs royalties on her books. The bestsellers usually do.

Established writers also follow a rule that Dean Wesley Smith and I teach our writing students: *Money flows to the writer.*

In the traditional publishing model, writers do not spend a dime out of pocket. If you're in a traditional publishing model, and someone asks you to cough up money to read the book or publish the book, then that someone is scamming you.

Remember: This is the *traditional* publishing model.

If you decide to remain in that model, then always keep that rule foremost in your mind: *Money flows to the writer.*

However, this rule gets in the way when you are starting your own publishing business. Publishers spend money to ensure that a book comes out.

If you go into self-publishing, then you will need to spend some money to put your books on the market.

Too many writers confuse the traditional publishing model—in which the writer puts no money out of pocket—with the self-publishing company that they're starting. Any new business, which is what a publishing company is, spends money out-of-pocket. That's why many small businesses need capital to start up, whether that capital comes from small business loans or from investors or from the business owners' pocket.

It is this distinction between the rules that established writers are used to from the old traditional publishing model and the rules governing any small business that is causing so many established writers to give their work over to companies that charge them no upfront fee and a percentage of the earnings.

These writers think they're being clever because they aren't investing up front. In *all* of those cases, the writer is thinking like a writer stuck in the 20th century instead of like a person running her own small business. That mistake in thinking guarantees that they're going to overpay in the long run by factors of a hundred for a service that would only cost a few hundred dollars if the writer thought like a businessperson.

Traditional publishers have made it easy for established writers to concentrate *only* on the writing. If a writer self-publishes her backlist, she must concentrate on the business, as well, *even if she never does any of the actual publishing work.*

So, how do you go from a business model in which you're paid to do one job and do it well to a model in which you must pay to get a job done?

You need to figure out how to fund your transition.

A handful of established writers, such as those at Bookview Café, are bartering skills with each other. One with graphic design experience will trade a book cover design for another writer's copy editor skills. These co-ops are starting up in various genres. I don't participate (I'm not someone you want in your organization, rabble rouser that I am), but I know many writers who do and swear by this method.

Two different writers I spoke with on my trip to Los Angeles are seeking investors to fund their publishing companies. One of these companies will be a self-publishing company and the other a more traditional publishing company. The self-publishing company is owned by a big name, so there's a built-in market that will entice investors.

But most savvy writers are paying for the covers and edits out of their own pockets. They're paying the flat fee as a start-up expense to get their self-publishing business off the ground.

Some of these writers have day jobs. Others are bestsellers with the money to invest. (One such writer, when I told him the fees he would face to self-publish a thriller he wrote, called the fees "pocket change." To me, the money was significant. To him, it was a sum he barely had to think about.)

However, most established writers run out of money long before the next check comes in. Yes, that writer's house is probably paid off and she probably paid cash for her car. But she's waiting for the next part of her advance to give her a cushion again.

That writer is easily tempted by these no-money-up-front percentage services.

And those are the writers who can least afford those services. If the writer put out a few hundred up front, she would be making a profit within a year, instead of losing 50%

or more of her earnings to a company that might or might not accurately report the income.

So, how does this type of writer afford the fees? Contact one of the companies that will provide a menu of services for a flat fee, and then figure out which services she'll need. See how much money it will take to publish that backlist book, *and then, save up for it.*

Because, remember, most established writers have time. They have time to save money, time to research the services they need to hire, time to compare prices and benefits.

I know some of you who are older mentioned that you're feeling the press of time because of health and life issues. Still, I would recommend that you go about this change methodically and that you document all that you've found so that the people who will help with your writing business down the road understand your plans.

In fact, everyone should do a variation on this, because we all will leave our writing businesses to our heirs one day—and we don't get to choose that day. That day might be tomorrow, no matter how old we are.

Many established writers, including me, are combining traditional publishing with self-publishing. We have backlist that's been out of print for a while and are putting it up ourselves.

We have a secondary transition to make, one that happens in the way we think about what we do.

Let's talk money first. With self-publishing, the writer moves from an advance model that pays in large lump sums every six months or so to a model in which a little bit of money comes in every month, which is much more like a paycheck.

The writer, used to getting thousands of dollars per check, will often think a few hundred per month is a tiny amount of money. But it's not when multiplied over a decade. Because the self-published book never has to go out of print unlike most traditionally published books.

Traditionally published books only stay on bookstore shelves for a few months at most. Even bestsellers with large backlists only see their most recent five or six books on a bookstore shelf in any given month. E-books are changing that dramatically. Books never leave the virtual shelf.

So, when calculating a book's earnings, the self-published writer can look at the income as it will accrue over years instead of months. Suddenly, earning $500 per month becomes a much better number. That's $6000 per year or $60,000 over ten years.

The more books and stories you have available, the more chances a reader has to find you. If your books come from multiple sources, like traditional publishing houses and your own self-publishing company, then all the better. Traditional publishing will get you into markets you can't get to yourself and, oddly enough, self-publishing now puts you in markets that your traditional publisher can't.

(For example, my most recent traditionally published novel, *City of Ruins*, didn't have an e-book edition for months after the print edition came out. Even when the e-book edition came out, it wasn't available in all English-speaking countries. Only in North America. Yet when I self-publish an e-book, it goes out worldwide. That's a change from just a few years ago.)

Established writers who have the luxury of time—and that's most of you—need to plan for the future now. Plan everything from how you want to proceed from here forward. Figure out if you want to be entirely published by traditional houses or if you want to self-publish some projects that traditional houses won't take. Figure out if you want to self-publish your backlist, and if you do, how hands-on you want to be.

Save money so that you can afford flat-fee services. Do what other small business owners do and comparison shop. Don't just go with a friend who happens to have an e-pub business. Make sure that she provides the best deal and the best work for the price.

And plan for change no matter what route you chose. Your agent may retire. Your publishing company might decline to take your next book. You might hit the *New York Times* bestseller list with a series in which half the books are out of print. (This happens to mystery writers all the time.) If that's the case, decide *beforehand* if it would be better to sell your backlist to a traditional publisher or do the work yourself.

Ask yourself all of these questions and more. The good questions—"what happens if I become a bestseller?"—to the bad questions—"what happens if my traditional publisher goes out of business tomorrow?" Answer those questions honestly.

You don't have to show those answers to anyone other than yourself.

Figure out what you want to do, how you will survive the good and the bad, and, most importantly, what you envision for your career five years down the road.

Once you have the answers written down, start planning. Set goals. Not just work goals, but financial goals as well.

Figure out how you can attain those goals. Figure out how you can afford to pay upfront on some backlist self-publishing without taking time from your writing or much-needed income from your household. Figure out what you'd do if you find yourself in a situation, like so many established writers often are, when your next book won't sell to any traditional publisher. Figure out how you'll handle your money if your most recent novel becomes a number one *New York Times* bestseller.

Now's the time to think about the future. Publishing is changing, and whether you like it or not, your writing career will change with it. Do what you can to be prepared. If you have the time, do the research. Plan. Make smart decisions.

Don't just do what everyone else is doing. Do what's best for you.

About the Author

Award-winning, bestselling writer Kristine Kathryn Rusch has published books under many names and in many genres. She has owned several businesses, and has worked for herself for more than thirty years. For more information on her work, go to kristinekathrynrusch.com.

If you found this short book helpful, you might want to read these books as well:

The Freelancer's Survival Guide
Getting Started
Goals and Dreams
How To Make Money
Networking in Person And Online
Time Management
The Secrets of Success
Turning Setbacks into Opportunity
When to Quit Your Day Job

More Business Books by

Kristine Kathryn Rusch

The Freelancer's Survival Guide (full book)

Freelancer's Survival Guide Short Books

When to Quit Your Day Job
Getting Started
Turning Setbacks into Opportunity
Goals and Dreams
How to Negotiate Anything
The Secrets of Success
How to Make Money
Networking in Person and Online
Time Management

Made in the USA
Charleston, SC
24 April 2012